This edition published in 2011 by:

The Rosen Publishing Group, Inc.
29 East 21st Street
New York, NY 10010

Additional end matter copyright © 2011 by The Rosen Publishing Group, Inc.

Library of Congress Cataloging-in-Publication Data

Chilman-Blair, Kim.
Medikidz explain autism / Kim Chilman-Blair and John Taddeo.
    p. cm. -- (Superheroes on a medical mission)
"Medical content reviewed for accuracy by Professor Simon Baron-Cohen and Dr. David Skuse."
Includes bibliographical references and index.
ISBN 978-1-4358-9460-0 (library binding) -- ISBN 978-1-4488-1835-8 (pbk.) -- ISBN 978-1-4488-1836-5 (6-pack)
1. Autism in children--Comic books, strips, etc. 2. Autism--Comic books, strips, etc. I. Taddeo, John. II. Title.
RJ506.A9C455 2011
618.92'85882--dc22

                2010008830

Manufactured in China

CPSIA Compliance Information: Batch #MS0102YA: For further information, contact Rosen Publishing, New York, New York, at 1-800-237-9932.

OCCIPITAL LOBE

PARIETAL LOBE

FRONTAL LOBE

TEMPORAL LOBE

...WELCOME TO THE BRAIN!

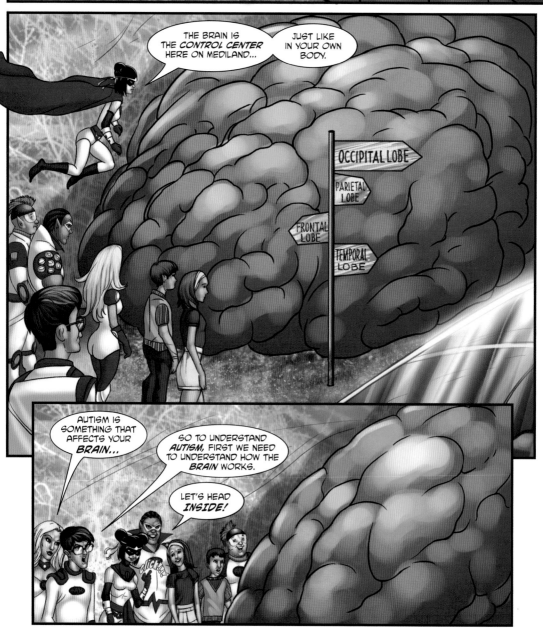

THE BRAIN IS THE *CONTROL CENTER* HERE ON MEDILAND...

JUST LIKE IN YOUR OWN BODY.

OCCIPITAL LOBE

PARIETAL LOBE

FRONTAL LOBE

TEMPORAL LOBE

AUTISM IS SOMETHING THAT AFFECTS YOUR *BRAIN*...

SO TO UNDERSTAND *AUTISM*, FIRST WE NEED TO UNDERSTAND HOW THE *BRAIN* WORKS.

LET'S HEAD *INSIDE!*

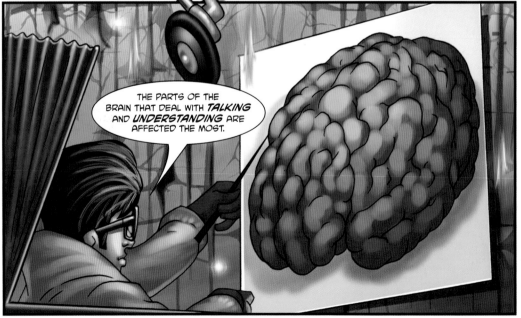

GLOSSARY

ANNOY TO MAKE A PERSON FEEL IMPATIENT OR
      SOMEWHAT ANGRY.

AUTISM A COMPLEX NEUROLOGICAL DISORDER THAT
      CAUSES PROBLEMS WITH VERBAL AND NONVERBAL
      COMMUNICATION AND SOCIAL INTERACTION.

BICEPS A MUSCLE THAT HAS TWO POINTS OF ATTACHMENT
      AT ONE END, IN PARTICULAR THE LARGE MUSCLE OF
      THE FRONT OF THE UPPER ARM.

BODY LANGUAGE THE MANNERISMS, GESTURES, AND
      FACIAL EXPRESSIONS OF THE BODY THAT CAN
      BE INTERPRETED AS UNCONSCIOUSLY COMMUNICATING
      SOMEONE'S FEELINGS OR MENTAL STATE.

BRAIN THE CENTER OF THE HUMAN NERVOUS SYSTEM.
      IT CONTROLS THOUGHT, INVOLUNTARY MOVEMENT
      IN THE BODY, BALANCE, GROWTH, AND TEMPERATURE
      CONTROL.

CLUMSY POORLY COORDINATED OR LACKING GRACE.

DEVELOPMENTAL DISORDER ONE OF SEVERAL
      DISORDERS, SUCH AS AUTISM OR DYSLEXIA, THAT
      APPEAR IN CHILDHOOD AND THAT INTERRUPT
      NORMAL DEVELOPMENT IN ONE OR MORE
      PSYCHOLOGICAL FUNCTIONS, LIKE LANGUAGE SKILLS.

DIAGNOSE TO IDENTIFY AN ILLNESS OR DISORDER IN
      A PATIENT THROUGH A PHYSICAL EXAM, INTERVIEW,
      OR MEDICAL TEST.

DISMISSED IN THE SPORT OF CRICKET, WHEN THE
      BATSMAN IS OUT.

DNA A SUBSTANCE CARRYING AN ORGANISM'S GENETIC
      INFORMATION. IT REPRODUCES ITSELF AND IS THE
      MEANS BY WHICH HEREDITARY TRAITS PASS FROM
      ONE GENERATION TO THE NEXT.

EMOTION A STRONG FEELING ABOUT SOMEONE OR
      SOMETHING.

FACIAL EXPRESSION THE LOOK ON SOMEONE'S FACE
      THAT REVEALS A PARTICULAR EMOTION.

GENETIC OF OR RELATING TO GENES OR HEREDITY.

IMPRESSIVE CAUSING ADMIRATION AND RESPECT;
      HAVING A DEEP AND USUALLY FAVORABLE OPINION
      ABOUT SOMEONE OR SOMETHING.

INFECTION A DISEASE THAT IS CATCHING; AN INFECTING
      MICROORGANISM.

INNER EAR THE FLUID-FILLED INTERNAL PART OF THE EAR,
        INCLUDING THE COCHLEA, WHICH IS RESPONSIBLE FOR
HEARING, AND THE SEMICIRCULAR CANALS, WHICH
        CONTROL A PERSON'S BALANCE.
MORPH TO TRANSFORM QUICKLY.
MUSIC THERAPY A TREATMENT IN PSYCHOTHERAPY IN
        WHICH A PATIENT IS ENCOURAGED TO USE SOUNDS
        AND SINGING TO RELIEVE EMOTIONS, OR IN WHICH
        MUSIC IS USED AS A TREATMENT.
NEURONS CELLS OF THE NERVOUS SYSTEM THAT ARE
        SPECIALIZED TO CARRY "MESSAGES" TO AND FROM
        THE BRAIN AND TO OTHER PARTS OF THE BODY.
RENEGOTIATE TO NEGOTIATE (SETTLE) SOMETHING AGAIN
        TO CHANGE THE ORIGINAL AGREED UPON TERMS.
SARCASM REMARKS THAT MEAN THE OPPOSITE OF WHAT
        THEY SEEM TO MEAN AND ARE INTENDED TO OFFEND
        SOMEONE.
SEVERE EXTREMELY BAD OR DANGEROUS.
SPECIALIST A MEDICAL DOCTOR WHO PRACTICES IN A
        SPECIFIC FIELD, SUCH AS A PEDIATRICIAN (WHO
        CARES FOR CHILDREN).
SPECTRUM DISORDER WHEN A CONDITION, SUCH AS
        AUTISM, AFFECTS PEOPLE DIFFERENTLY IT IS CALLED
        A SPECTRUM DISORDER. TWO INDIVIDUALS WITH THE
        SAME SPECTRUM DISORDER MIGHT NOT HAVE THE
        SAME BEHAVIOR OR SKILLS.
SYMPTOM A PHYSICAL OR MENTAL FEATURE THAT
        INDICATES A CONDITION OF A DISEASE OR OTHER
        DISORDER, ESPECIALLY ONE EXPERIENCED BY
        THE PATIENT; FOR EXAMPLE, IF A PERSON FEELS PAIN,
        DIZZINESS, OR ITCHING.
THERAPIST SOMEONE TRAINED TO TREAT DISORDERS,
        ESPECIALLY A PERSON WHO USES METHODS OTHER
        THAN DRUGS AND SURGERY.
TOXIC CHEMICALS POISONOUS, HARMFUL, OR DEADLY
        SUBSTANCES.

FOR MORE INFORMATION

AMERICAN PSYCHOLOGICAL ASSOCIATION
750 FIRST STREET NE
WASHINGTON, DC 20002-4242
(800) 374-2721
WEB SITE: HTTP://WWW.APA.ORG/TOPICS/AUTISM/INDEX.ASPX
THIS ORGANIZATION PROVIDES INFORMATION ON PSYCHOLOGICAL
        DISEASES AND ON AUTISM; ITS WEB SITE HAS A SPECIAL
        SECTION FOR STUDENTS (HTTP://WWW.APA.ORG/ABOUT/
        STUDENTS.ASPX).

AUTISM CANADA FOUNDATION
P.O. BOX 366
BOTHWELL, ON NOP 1CO
CANADA
(519) 695-5858
WEB SITE: HTTP://WWW.AUTISMCANADA.ORG
THE FOUNDATION SUPPORTS CANADIANS BY GIVING INFORMATION
        ABOUT BIOMEDICAL AND BEHAVIORAL TREATMENT TO HELP
        THOSE AFFECTED BY AUTISM.

AUTISM SOCIETY OF AMERICA
4340 EAST-WEST HIGHWAY, SUITE 350
BETHESDA, MD 20814
(800) 328-8476
WEB SITE: HTTP://WWW.AUTISM-SOCIETY.ORG
THIS ORGANIZATION PROVIDES INFORMATION ON ALL ASPECTS OF
        AUTISM, INCLUDING VALUABLE ADVICE ON LIVING AND COPING
        WITH THE DISORDER.

AUTISM SOCIETY OF CANADA (ASC)
BOX 22017
1670 HERON ROAD
OTTAWA, ON K1V OC2
CANADA
(866) 476-8440
WEB SITE: HTTP://WWW.AUTISMSOCIETYCANADA.CA
ASC IS A CANADIAN NONPROFIT CHARITABLE ORGANIZATION THAT IS
        COMMITTED TO PUBLIC EDUCATION AND INFORMATION ABOUT
        AUTISM AND TRIES TO REDUCE THE IMPACT ON FAMILIES WHO
        ARE AFFECTED BY AUTISM AND ASPERGER'S SYNDROME.

NATIONAL INSTITUTE OF NEUROLOGICAL DISORDERS AND STROKE
(NINDS)
NATIONAL INSTITUTES OF HEALTH
C/O NIH NEUROLOGICAL INSTITUTE
P.O. BOX 5801
BETHESDA, MARYLAND 20824
(800) 352-9424
WEB SITE: HTTP://WWW.NINDS.NIH.GOV/DISORDERS/AUTISM/DETAIL_
AUTISM.HTM
A PART OF THE NATIONAL INSTITUTES OF HEALTH, NINDS CONDUCTS

AND SUPPORTS RESEARCH ON BRAIN AND NERVOUS SYSTEM DISORDERS. AN AUTISM FACT SHEET IS AVAILABLE ON ITS WEB PAGE.

TALK ABOUT CURING AUTISM (TACA)
3070 BRISTOL STREET, SUITE 340
COSTA MESA, CA 92626
(949) 640-4401
WEB SITE: HTTP://WWW.TACANOW.COM/CONTACTUS.HTM
THIS IS AN ORGANIZATION THAT PROVIDES INFORMATION AND
        SUPPORT TO FAMILIES AND COMMUNITIES AFFECTED BY AUTISM.

U.S. AUTISM AND ASPERGER ASSOCIATION
P.O. BOX 532
DRAPER, UT 84020-0532
(888) 928-8476)
WEB SITE: HTTP://WWW.USAUTISM.ORG
THIS NONPROFIT ORGANIZATION FOR AUTISM AND ASPERGER'S
        SYNDROME PROVIDES EDUCATION, SUPPORT, AND RESOURCES
        TO PEOPLE WHO ARE AFFECTED BY AUTISM SPECTRUM
        DISORDERS.

U.S. CENTERS FOR DISEASE CONTROL AUTISM SPECTRUM DISORDERS
1600 CLIFTON ROAD
ATLANTA, GA 30333
(800) 232-4636
WEB SITE: HTTP://WWW.CDC.GOV/NCBDDD/AUTISM/INDEX.HTML
THIS AGENCY PROVIDES INFORMATION ON AUTISM SPECTRUM
        DISORDERS AND RESOURCES FOR FAMILIES.

WEB SITES

DUE TO THE CHANGING NATURE OF INTERNET LINKS, ROSEN PUBLISHING HAS DEVELOPED AN ONLINE LIST OF WEB SITES RELATED TO THE SUBJECT OF THIS BOOK. THIS SITE IS UPDATED REGULARLY. PLEASE USE THIS LINK TO ACCESS THIS LIST:

HTTP://WWW.ROSENLINKS.COM/MED/AUTI

ALLMAN, TONY. *AUTISM (DISEASES AND DISORDERS)*. DETROIT, MI: LUCENT BOOKS, 2009.

BAKER, JEFF. *PREPARING FOR LIFE: THE COMPLETE GUIDE FOR TRANSITIONING TO ADULTHOOD FOR THOSE WITH AUTISM AND ASPERGER'S SYNDROME*. ARLINGTON, TX: FUTURE HORIZONS, 2006.

BARDHAN-QUALLEN, SUDIPTA. *AUTISM (UNDERSTANDING DISEASES AND DISORDERS)*. DETROIT, MI: KIDHAVEN PRESS, 2005.

BONNICE, SHERRY. *HIDDEN CHILD: YOUTH WITH AUTISM*. BROOMALL, PA: MASON CREST PUBLISHERS, 2004.

FLEISCHER, LEONORE, KIERAN MCGOVERN, AND BOB HARVEY. *RAIN MAN*. NEW YORK, NY: PENGUIN, 2000.

FREDERICKS, CARRIE. *AUTISM (PERSPECTIVES ON DISEASES AND DISORDERS)*. DETROIT, MI: GREENHAVEN PRESS, 2007.

GRANDIN, TEMPLE, AND KATE DUFFY. *DEVELOPING TALENTS: CAREERS FOR INDIVIDUALS WITH ASPERGER SYNDROME AND HIGH-FUNCTIONING AUTISM*. SHAWNEE MISSION, KS: AUTISM ASPERGER PUBLISHING CO., 2004.

GRANDIN, TEMPLE, AND SEAN BARRON. *THE UNWRITTEN RULES OF SOCIAL RELATIONSHIPS: DECODING SOCIAL MYSTERIES THROUGH THE UNIQUE PERSPECTIVES OF AUTISM*. ARLINGTON, TX: FUTURE HORIZONS, 2006.

MEYERS, KAREN H. *THE TRUTH ABOUT ADHD AND OTHER NEUROBIOLOGICAL DISORDERS* (THE TRUTH ABOUT). NEW YORK, NY: FACTS ON FILE, 2010.

RODRIGUEZ, ANA MARIA. *AUTISM AND ASPERGER SYNDROME* (TWENTY-FIRST CENTURY MEDICAL LIBRARY). MINNEAPOLIS, MN: TWENTY-FIRST CENTURY BOOKS, 2009.

ROSALER, MAXINE. *COPING WITH ASPERGER SYNDROME*. NEW YORK, NY: ROSEN PUBLISHING GROUP, INC., 2004.

SHORE, STEPHEN, AND G. RASTELLIS. *UNDERSTANDING AUTISM FOR DUMMIES*. INDIANAPOLIS, IN: FOR DUMMIES/JOHN WILEY, 2006.

TURKINGTON, CAROL, AND RUTH ANAN. *THE ENCYCLOPEDIA OF AUTISM SPECTRUM DISORDERS* (LIBRARY OF HEALTH AND LIVING). NEW YORK, NY: FACTS ON FILE, 2006.

VEAGUE, HEATHER BARNETT. *AUTISM (PSYCHOLOGICAL DISORDERS)*. NEW YORK, NY: CHELSEA HOUSE PUBLISHERS, 2009.

INDEX

ABOUT THE AUTHORS

DR. KIM CHILMAN-BLAIR IS A MEDICAL DOCTOR WITH TEN YEARS OF EXPERIENCE IN MEDICAL WRITING AND A PASSION FOR PROVIDING MEDICAL INFORMATION THAT MAKES CHILDREN WANT TO LEARN.

JOHN TADDEO, FORMALLY OF MARVEL ENTERTAINMENT, IS A CELEBRATED COMIC BOOK WRITER AND DIRECTOR OF TWO AWARD-WINNING ANIMATED SHORTS.